Of an island I love
And visited with the woman I love

Christmas 2009

Jh

SICILY

A MEETING OF MEDITERRANEAN CIVILIZATIONS

WHITE STAR
PUBLISHERS

SICILY

A MEETING OF MEDITERRANEAN CIVILIZATIONS

The pictures on these pages give an initial impression of the island of Sicily. They show the Greek theater of Segesta, salt lakes formed by the sea and the sand at Cape Tindari, the ancient temples in Agrigento, the hellish, Dantesque atmosphere of an eruption on Mount Etna, and the green riot of citrus trees and ancient palms before the impressive temple architecture. Also shown are the church of Santa Rosalia in Palermo, the processions of the hooded monks of the confraternities at Easter, and the sacrifice of the tuna-god in the tuna-killing season off Favignana. Sacred and profane, splendid and dreadful, gentle and violent, Sicily is marked by a taste defined by Goethe as "Palagonian."

Text
Giuseppe Lazzaro Danzuso

Photographs
Giulio Veggi

Graphic design
Patrizia Balocco Lovisetti

Translation
C.T.M., Milan

CONTENTS

The Editor wishes to thank **IGM** SpA and its associated companies within Gruppo Waste Management for valuable help in producing this book.

ISBN 88-8095-776-7

Reprints:
1 2 3 4 5 6   06 05 04 03 02

Printed in Italy

2-3 Segesta: Greek theater.

4-5 Agrigento: Concordia Temple.

6-7 Tindari: salt lakes formed by the sand.

8-9 Etna: volcanic eruption.

10 Agrigento: Temple of the Dioscuri.

11 Palermo: Church of Santa Rosalia.

12-13 Calatafimi: Festival of the Crucifix.

14-15 Favignana: tuna killing.

A "PALAGONIAN" ISLAND

It would certainly be presumptuous to try to describe Sicily in a single book because even the smallest of the 420 communes of the island (the largest region in Italy) has such a vast historical, architectural, cultural and natural wealth that it alone would merit a volume. And so as not to reduce this book to a long and dry series of lists, the only choice possible is to paint the island with broad brush-strokes, picking out the occasional detail in discussions of monuments, traditional activities, the people and their legends in order to give an idea of the atmosphere of Sicily, the island in which, according to Johann Wolfgang Goethe, "lies the key to everything." "Italy without Sicily," wrote the great German at the end of the 18th century, "leaves no image in the soul." And one cannot but share Goethe's feeling if one considers that this island represented not the demarcation line but the point of contact and fusion of many Mediterranean cultures. It is, in Goethe's words, "a marvellous center where the many spokes of universal history converge."

What makes Sicily fascinating is its unique blend of cultures and races created by the lure, since prehistoric times, of its mild climate, fertile land and strategic position. Many peoples were induced to climb aboard this enormous ship berthed at the center of the Mediterranean; of the native people, we know almost nothing except for the remains in the cave of Uzzo and those, even more ancient, of a delicate race of Australopithecus hominids that lived in the area around Agrigento between five million and three and a half million years ago when Sicily was still attached to Tunisia. Apart from the Elimo tribe, the first people we know of settled beneath the great mountain that spits flame. These were the Sicans, who probably reached the island on giant rafts from Iberia. They chose the area around Mount Etna because the black sand that spouts from the volcano makes the surrounding soil so fertile. But 1500 years before Christ, according to Diodorus, the Sicans fled to the west of the island as a result of a particularly frightening eruption. This left space for the Siculi tribe who arrived from Lazio in mainland Italy several millennia after the arrival of the Sicani. It was Italo, king of the Siculi, that the peninsula was named after. The Siculi (who probably belonged to the same ethnic group as the Sicani) passed across the Strait of Messina on skins filled with air and built Sicily's first metropolis, below the volcano. The remains of the settlement – encircled by towers, inhabited by 2000 people and boasting a temple dedicated to a god named Adranon that personified Etna, the lord of fire and war – can still be seen on the banks of the river Simeto. It was here that the first and only inscription in the language of the people who gave their name to the island has been found. The Siculi also built Pantalica, Europe's largest prehistoric necropolis containing 5000 tombs excavated in sheer rock faces. Excavation must have been a titanic task considering that they were dug out before the discovery of iron.

Next the Greeks arrived; they built cities, temples and theaters, they imported olives, pistachios and vines and enriched the pottery art of the Siculi. Then there were the Phoenicians who left immense dry-docks, mosaics and exotic idols. Later, of course, the Romans arrived. They made the island into an immense granary and built splendid villas and palaces adorned with statues. Following the Romans came the Byzantines, who built Cube and other rock churches and transformed the sanctuary of Athena into Syracuse's first cathedral and the Concordia Temple in Agrigento into a church. The Arabs followed and left a legacy of mosques, minarets and such lovely Gardens of Delight that Count Roger the Norman regretted having destroyed them. The Arabs also created a new culture of agriculture, cooking and handcrafts; they divided the island into three valleys and married the snows of Etna to the juice of citrus fruits and honey to create delicious sorbets. Following the Normans, the Swabians arrived. They built hundreds of castles and towers, some from black lava, and strengthened the local wines by teaching the islanders how to cultivate the vines on the faces of the hills most exposed to the sun.

Then the French – the Angevins – arrived once more. With them the Gothic architecture of the Chiaramonte family flourished, prompting the construction of Palazzo Steri in Palermo but also causing the famed Sicilian Vespers War. The Aragonese from Spain became the dominant power. They married Catalan Gothic to Chiaramonte Gothic and introduced Baroque architecture when rebuilding towns destroyed by earthquakes. Their versions of religious ceremonies also left a lasting mark on local Catholic rites. Centuries later, the English arrived. They neither invaded nor colonized; their only aim was to produce port on Sicilian soil and thus they created the Marsala wine district in western Sicily. Finally, the Americans moved into the NATO bases in eastern Sicily, on the heels of jazz and John Wayne movies.

The result is that today Sicily is like an amazing machine that can take you back and forth in time and space: to the dawn of the human world via a volcanic eruption, to prehistoric tombs from 5000 years ago, to an exotic scene like that of the papyrus on the river Ciane, to the snowy silver firs in the Petralian hills. Modern Sicilians are the result of this rich social mix from the past, also of peoples who have come to the island seeking refuge in more recent times, for example, the Albanians who fled during the 15th century in the face of a Turkish invasion and created a community in which their ancient rites are still handed down; and

descendants of Lombards called by Count Roger to an area between Etna and the Nebrodi hills that still speak an ancient Gallic-Italian dialect. All these peoples exist within the traditions and customs of modern Sicilians because different experiences and different ways of understanding existence and the relationship between the divine and nature have fused to give life to a single culture that differs from all those that contributed to it. Although we often do not give the respect due to what is dissimilar, this culture is founded on differences – ones sometimes even extraordinary. And the greatest marvel to the strict and rational travelers who "explored" Sicily in the late 18th and early 19th centuries was the lack of conflict that existed between local tastes, languages and traditions. I think it is important to analyze the writings of such travelers – ten Frenchmen, six Germans, six Britons, two Danes, one Swiss, one Pole and one Russian – in their descriptions of a Sicily past but ready to re-emerge before our eyes as if two hundred years had passed in the twinkling of an eye. It is important because, as Vincenzo Consolo points out, these people "gave visibility to what, for Sciascia, previously was invisible to Sicilians." The sensitivity of these travelers first made them hostile to and critical of the great confusion of styles and ruins that reigned on this island of wars and earthquakes. "Who can look without sorrow at these corpses of cities, these tombs of peoples?," wrote the son of the philosopher Jacobi who accompanied Stolberg in Sicily. Then they began to understand the sense of the contrasts when they reached Etna, the metaphor of the Sicilian microcosm, that breaks its apparent eternal quiet to liberate its pent-up energy with violence. The volcano destroys with its lava but turns fields into gardens with its black sand. It is a mountain that is paradise on the exterior but hell inside on which "the most delicate vegetation grows on blocks of spent fire," noted the German Johann Heinrich Bartels. It is Sicily's luxuriant growth that brings everything back to life. Another illuminating visit for the travelers was to the stone quarries of Syracuse, defined by Jacobi as "adventurous upsetting forms that bring to mind visions of an uncontrolled imagination." But in this place Bartels also saw how "the agile vine ties itself to the gigantic rock masses, between the fig trees and pomegranates that grow out of the stone," and the Frenchman Jean-Marie Roland de la Platière saw how the water had "formed a prodigious quantity of earthy stalactites that resemble petrified tree roots." Vivant Denon emphasized that what struck him about the place was "the contrast between the delicate and the terrible." This contrast has been the model for Sicilian taste, which Bartels defined as "extraordinary and marvellous," and which is extolled in the "Villa of the Monsters" in Bagheria. Previously Goethe had not hidden his disapproval in Palermo where the buildings rose "at random and at whim" and where a prince had built a bizarre palazzo just outside the city with sculptures of monsters. Almost without exception the travelers considered this fascinating castle reprehensible and blasphemous. The disquiet that the Villa of the Monsters raised in these great minds and the space that they dedicated to it in their journals are symptomatic: unconsciously, they felt they had come across the root of a fundamental aspect of "Sicilianness." And it was Goethe who, with great intuition, created a neologism when he defined any manifestation of the Sicilian imagination as "Palagonian." Today we have only a vague idea of what the villa looked like as, after the death of the prince, his brother-in-law destroyed many of the "monsters," sculptures and ornaments that, the Briton Patrick Brydone and the Pole Borch recorded, so struck the imagination of pregnant women scared of bringing a monster into the world. Two drawings by Count Borch survive that show the balustrade covered with chimerae, demons and creatures part human, part animal.

One of the drawings shows a woman with the head of a horse playing cards with a gryphon dressed as a horseman. There were also hydras, monkeys playing music, emperors with two noses or the body of a dwarf, statues with clocks in that moved their eyes, wrinkled babies, busts of women devoured by insects, deforming mirrors, columns of tools stuck together and chandeliers made from pieces of broken bottles and glasses. A sort of "red thread" links Etna, the Alcantara gorges, the "Turkish Steps" at Realmonte, the stone quarries of Syracuse, the Santoni of Palazzolo Acreide, the Fort at Gagliano Castelferrato, the Baroque corbels of Palazzo Villadorata in Noto, the monumental cemetery at Caltagirone, the Villa of the Monsters and another bewitched castle, built at Sciacca in the early 1900s by Don Filippo Bentivegna known as Filippu di li testi (Filippo of the heads). And a "red thread" also clearly emerges at any large popular Sicilian festival: Santa Rosalia in Palermo, Sant'Agata in Catania or Sant'Alfio in Trecastagni. All are manifestations which express the ability of Sicilians to transform a stall into a palace, a bandstand into a princely castle or a cart into a firmament of stars, even with little or few means. These festivals show the desire of the Sicilian people to express themselves through elaborate architecture or decorations whether made from marble or cardboard. Also because, given the violence of the earthquakes that strike this island, no one knows which material might be the more resistant at the time. And while on the subject of festivals, as in many American and Australian cities these are perpetuated in miniature by the Sicilians who live there, it is worthwhile to discuss another fact that will help complete this

19 *A picture of a small street in Erice, one that might have been taken in any old Sicilian village. The crooked street has grass growing between the cobbles and moss on the walls of the houses which were built to fit the shape of the mountain side. On the festival of the village's patron saint, the houses are hung with flowers and flags.*

fundamental portrait of the island and its inhabitants: what it is that has made Sicily expand beyond its confines through emigration. *Giuseppe Tomaso di Lampedusa*, author of the novel The Leopard, recalls how the islanders considered themselves to be the "salt of the earth" and, in part, they have been and are. It is as if the children of all those peoples who over the millennia have landed on the ship moored in the Mediterranean and contaminated by poverty had decided to disembark; not just in their countries of origin but also in new and distant lands, taking with them their pride, the skills of their hands and minds and a cardboard suitcase filled with olive oil, wine and bread, the simplest expressions of a culture thousands of years old.

It is clear that Sicily cannot be considered simply an island. It is a continent in miniature, a melting pot of races, cultures, languages and religions. For this reason experiments of great importance have been carried out here over the centuries in the fields of democracy and civil coexistence. The first was by Roger de Hauteville in the year 1000 AD, which left the defeated Arabs in charge of administration of the bureaucracy and so created the first multi-racial society in the world in which Catholics, Orthodox Christians, Moslems and Jews lived peacefully together, divided only by the color of their skins and their houses: white, yellow, blue and pale pink. These colors have survived in the smallest coastal and inland villages, handed down by tradition though the colors themselves have long lost their original significance.

Other examples also show how Sicily has been at the forefront socially and politically: the first island parliament, the plaques describing citizens' rights in Sciacca in the 18th century, the socialist municipalism of Giuseppe De Felice in 19th century Catania and the Catholic municipalism of Don Sturzo in Caltagirone in the 20th century. In addition, over the centuries models of production were drawn up that may have been unsophisticated but were respectful of the environment; a learned culture was formed that ranged from Giulio d'Alcamo to Pirandello, Sciascia, Bufalino and a popular culture raised on a taste for beauty that did not preclude any types of style and which found its maximum expression via architectural craftsmen.

When the backwardness of Sicily is discussed, what is not taken into consideration is that the island is an enormous laboratory which the world can watch to understand the development of certain phenomena, such as the Mafia. It is in Sicily that, in the age of the global village, the whole world can discover – ways to free itself from such monsters – which already are beginning to run free in the rest of Italy and the world. And, again, it is from this island at the center of the Old World that a universal lesson might be learned of civil coexistence and peace under the flag of four colors: white, yellow, blue and pink.

*20 top Bagheria: Villa of
the Monsters.*

20-21 View of Noto.

*21 top Noto: Palazzo
Ducezio.*

*22-23 Hector's Salt-works,
adjacent to Mozia.*

*24-25 Madonie: the Targa
Florio road race.*

*26-27 Cultivated land in
Sicily's interior.*

CITIES, THE MARKS OF MAN

Sicilian cities leave their mark, either forcing you to love them wildly or to hate them – there are no half measures. They require long descriptions, like memories of a trip to an exotic island, to provide an exact idea of them. Many are now dead although they once played a great part in the development of civilization: Imera, Eloro, Solunto, Megara, Morgantina, Naxos, Gela, Adranon, Segesta, Selinunte, ancient Noto and a thousand others, with temples, theaters, castles, houses, wells, roads and fortifications that recount a section of Sicilian history, just as those that are still alive embrace the traces of the past. It happens at Agrigento, where, in the words of Pirandello who was born there, the hill-top city is surrounded by "a landscape of Saracen olive trees that faces the edges of a plateau of blue clay on the African sea" and overlooks the Valley of the Temples, dressed with almond trees. On summer nights the valley becomes a single temple: the visitor sits in religious silence beneath the immense sky sprinkled with stars, enjoying the psalmodizing of the crickets and the smells of the plants wafted by the sea breeze, and caresses the columns made from shell tufa to understand the secret that transforms them at each sunrise into pure gold. It happens at Syracuse, built from blindingly white stone. Living stone, like that of Euralio Castle and the legendary walls of Dennis that were raised in twenty days by sixty thousand men and twelve thousand oxen, endorsements of the immense strength of the peoples that built these colossal monuments. Like the Greek theater, one of the largest in the world, where ancient Greek tragedies that demonstrate the immutability of man's feelings are re-enacted. This is also the city of cut rock, of the Ear of Dionysius with its worrying echoes, and of the Cave of the Rope-makers. And of course of the magnificent marbles in the Archaeological Museum, like the Landolina Venus and other masterpieces.

But there is also the Syracuse of the cathedral, which promises you respite from the heat and then traps you with its beauties, of the island of the Ortygia on spring afternoons that evoke legends like that of the nymph Arethusa who was turned into the spring of the Ciane river, where papyrus grows naturally. Then there is the papyrus itself, reduced to archaic and arcane paper by the Naro sisters, custodians of the mysteries of their ancestor Landolina.

And then there is Palermo, all blood and emotion, regal and popular, with its open dialect and picturesque phraseology. "*Pani schittu e Cassaru*" is used to describe the purebred Palermitan – he who has drunk water from the ancient spring of the Garaffo river – ready to renounce everything just to "*ammulari i balati,*" i.e., wear down the wide paving slabs in the Corso (the Corso is called the Cassaro because there was once an Arab castle there). If during the evening stroll (inevitably called the *cassariata*) one passes a woman showing more than she should, she may be spoken of as "*una di chiddi di lu Chianu di la Curti,*" referring to the statues of the naked women adorning the fountain in Pretoria Square, once known as Piano della Corte. This enormous 16th-century fountain also contains statues of men whom the Messinesi disfigured by hacking off their noses. As the punishment at the time for pimps was having one's nose cut, the Messinesi considered the comparison a good one. But the poor girl above might also be as ugly as "*La Morti di lu Spitali,*" (the dead in the hospital) which refers to a 15th-century fresco painted during a restoration of Palazzo Sclafani, which was later transformed into a hospital. A quarrel is compared to the "*Curtigghiu di li Raunisi*" (courtyard of the Aragonese), where the commoners were always ready to "*far sciarra*" (argue) with the sellers. Yelling is also called *vucciria*, not for the assonance with the Italian verb "vociare" but for the name of the main market in Palermo, the *vucci* which means butchers.

A tall passerby is referred to as "*autu quantu la culonna di Sannuminicu*" (tall as the column of San Domenico), which was put up in the square of the church of San Domenico in 1726 to support the bronze statue of the Virgin Mary. Particularly lively children are compared, with an exaggerated anger, to "*Diavuli di la Zisa*" which refers to a 13th-century castle built in Arabic-Norman style in the Palermitan quarter of Zesa which depicts a great confusion of *putti* on the ceiling of the arched vault; the confusion is so great that, legend says, it is impossible to count them and they are considered little devils. And when one loses one's patience – according to the folklorist Giuseppe Pitré who collected more than 14,000 proverbs, mottoes and phrases at the beginning of the century – a rather indecent phrase describes one as "*avilli quantu la cubbula di San Giulianu*" ("having balls as big as the dome of San Giuliano" where size is an indication of the extent of one's anger). The huge dome only exists in the memory of the Palermitan people as it was destroyed to make room for the Teatro Massimo.

In Catania, the *Cassaro* is the Via Etnea which "is the incarnation of the very tip of vanity, like an honorary citizenship," wrote Riccardo Bacchelli. It is miles long and painted in bright colors by Antonio Aniante: "... it is the most famous ice-cream factory in the world and it is only authentic in summer: when the stars in the Catania sky are the largest and brightest in the firmament and the jasmine flowers that climb over the soft drink stalls are as large and plump as a child's hand." The old city center surrounds the Via Etnea with the Via dei Crociferi which, remembers Carlo Levi, "has a mysterious charm at night, with its churches and the arch, even if the headless horse no longer wanders around as it used to during the nights of the 18th century." Then there is the Castello Ursino which "looks at the sea from which the lava has separated it, the great face of the unfinished Benedictine black tower blacker than a black sky." The narrow perimeter of

the Baroque city center built after the terrible earthquake of 1693 contains many other remarkable things, like the Cathedral, built over the remains of the Achillean Baths and in front of the statue of the elephant, symbol of the city, carved from lava. The elephant is nicknamed "liotru" which is a corruption of the name of the mythical magician Heliodorus. Close by there is a fountain of an underground river, the Amenano, which stands in the colorful setting of the fish market, then there is a Greek theater, an Odeon, the house-cum-museum of Giovanni Verga and another of Vincenzo Bellini, the theater dedicated to the composer, the University and the *palazzo* that belonged to the Prince of Biscari. Finally there is the Bellini Garden which Jules Verne described as "one of the most beautiful in Europe with ... in the background, the superb volcano adorned with vapor."

In Messina, the background is the Calabrian coast because this city, destroyed by apocalyptic earthquakes in 1783 and 1908, is now characterized by low buildings. It was as if the port peninsula, known as St. Rainier's Scythe because of its shape, had rained blows down on the city to mow down victims of blood and stone. But the inhabitants of the city did not give in and in 1933, next to the Norman cathedral, built a bell-tower with the largest mechanical clock in the world, a symbol of their will. The clock is decorated with moving figures that represent historical and religious episodes. One of the figures is Death with scythe in hand which is intended to be both a warning and a commemoration of a resistance that is only for the strong. In order to comply with anti-seismic regulations during reconstruction after the last disaster, the new buildings had to be built low, and so that they might still have some exceptional feature to boast, the unknown craftsmen put all their efforts into the decorations with a taste that was fully "palagonian." In search of their lost architectural heritage, they first modelled columns, capitals, balustrades, corbels, fascias, panels, caryatids, gargoyles, flowers, fruit, dragons, *putti*, centaurs, chimerae, and every sort of monstrous animal using clay and chalk. They made moulds filled with cement and marble dust that were sacrificed with blows of a hammer when the decoration was finished.

Ragusa and her twin city Ibla were also born as the result of an earthquake and are the daughters of an ancient urban center. The two grew clinging onto the sides of contiguous hills joined by a series of steps and bridges, "wearing their Baroque with the reserve of an old lady," wrote Gesualdo Bufalino, who went on to say that, to visit Ibla, "a certain quality of spirit is required ... one professes a passion for architectural machinations where the fondness for airborne form hides, until the last, the *coup de thèatre* of the false perspective." This is the case with the masterpiece of Rosario Gagliardi, the master carpenter turned architect extraordinaire: Ibla cathedral, dedicated to St. George, represents a sort of "summa" of religious

30-31 One of the loveliest existing examples of Doric architecture, Segesta Temple has resisted the wear of time and destruction by the Vandals and the Arabs. The temple and the Greek theater are the only well-preserved buildings remaining in this ancient city, founded in prehistoric times and in one period inhabited by the Elimo people.

32-33 The Concordia
Temple (6th century BC)
seems almost whole
despite the fragility of the
shell tufa. It is the best
conserved Greek temple
after the Temple of
Theseus in Athens (made
from marble). Experts
believe that its survival is
due to the fact that it was
transformed into a three-
nave Christian church by
Gregory, the bishop of
Agrigento.

33 top left The Temple of
the Dioscuri was built
during the 5th century BC
and gravely damaged when
the city was destroyed by
the Carthaginians. It was
restored in later centuries.

33 top right This is what
remains of the Temple of
Hercules, the oldest in
Agrigento. It once had
thirty-eight columns and
was adorned with statues,
wall linings and paintings.

architecture in Sicily up till the end of the 18th century. At the top of a long flight of steps, its imposing facade appears ringed by a railing of iron lacework. The facade is so beautiful that it was nearly copied in a reconstruction of the nearby 16th-century church of San Giuseppe. Then there is the Ragusan version of Palagonian style with the grotesque figures and gargoyles on the Zacco, Consentini and Lupis *palazzi* which seem to represent figures from popular fables.

Standing on Frederick Swabian tower in the regal town of Enna, it is easy to understand why the Arabs thought of dividing up the island into three valleys. Enna is at the center of the island of three headlands and at times she hides herself from them in a veil of fog, just like a grand lady. Enna is the city where men do not feel the need to fly like birds because from here it seems possible to reach out and touch Etna. Enna is almost unassailable, like the Lombard Castle, having been built on a mountain from which parts of the slopes were cut away to prevent scaling, and the character of the inhabitants is the same - kind but distant - until their mouths open in a fraternal and winning smile signaling eternal friendship. It is a real treasure, like the one inside the cathedral with its rather shabby exterior: extraordinary pointed arches on basalt columns and a caisson ceiling of moving beauty and splendid fonts. There is another treasure chest with its precious jewels: the museum dedicated to Alessi that contains Sicily's religious masterpieces of the goldsmith's art. Confronted by the "Crown of the Madonna," the spectator is breathless with admiration. The Montalbano brothers from Palermo dedicated an entire year of work to create this perfect example of the prodigiousness of the Sicilians.

Caltanissetta, on the other hand, is a mixture of the smells of sulfur and ploughed fields. It has a museum dedicated to the sulfur mines that represented both the daily bread and the suffering of youngsters little more than children, who were painted by Onofrio Tomaselli breathless from the effort of transporting their loads of yellow rock in the palpable heat. They are so lifelike that you feel you could ask them about their red-haired companion, Ciaula. Caltanissetta is so obsessed with water that it built a 16th-century fountain with a bronze triton and seahorse right in front of the cathedral. This too is a Palagonian city to judge by the large anthropomorphic and zoomorphic corbels of the palace built by Count Luigi Moncada e Aragona in the 17th century. It is also small, poor and often forgotten though one of Sicily's best cultural lodes is to be found here, hidden behind its fortifications like the Pietrarossa castle that dominates the city.

And finally there is Trapani, the Trapani of the wind, the salt-mines, nautical beams, tuna-fishing and couscous. It is also the city of the Odyssey because it seems that Homer was born here – not in Greece – and he wasn't a man, but a woman, so much so that her

34 top The hexastyle Temple E at Selinunte dates from the 5th century BC.

34-35 Temple C at Selinunte was constructed during the first half of the 5th century BC.

35 top Important archaeological finds have recently been brought to light thanks to studies made at Villa Morgantina.

apprehension of the sea is made quite transparent in her work. Bradford and Butler and then Pococka have tried to rediscover the places along this coast where Odysseus lived his adventures. Trapani also has an Arab quarter around the port in which the principal roads are *shari*, the secondary roads are *darb*, and the alleyways and courtyards are *azzicca*. In the nearby quarter of Giudecca, the Spedaletto and the nearby tower were built with diamond-pointed ashlars. The *Santuario dell'Annunziata* (Sanctuary of the Annunciation) has a splendid rose window and a Gothic portal and, inside, there is the *Cappella dei Marinai* (Sailors' Chapel) and the statue of the "Madonna of Trapani" that stands over a silver model of the city. Near to the Sanctuary and its imposing Baroque bell-tower stands the monastery of the Annunciation that houses the museum with its "magnificent grand staircase." The museum contains a late-18th-century scene of the birth of Christ made entirely from coral which unites two of the city's traditional arts – the carving of coral and crib scenes – *toru* and *sangu*.

These cities that have been discussed are the provincial capitals but there are so many more extraordinary towns, for example, Taormina, the pearl that clings to the flanks of Mount Tauro with a splendid panorama over the sea and Etna, a glorious Greco-Roman amphitheater, the cathedral, and the Corvaja and Ciampoli palaces. There is also the medieval Erice, built inside a triangle - a foggy town that has been sacred to women for millennia and is now dedicated to science - and the Palagonian Noto, really just a large theater where the song of life is sung. Caltagirone, famous for pottery and its 142-step stairway; Monreale with its Norman cathedral and cloister with 228 decorated columns; Cefalù with another Norman cathedral and the *Portrait of an Unknown Man* by Antonello da Messina; Tindari, with its Greek theater that opens onto the sea and salt-water lakes that continually change shape, and from where one can see Lipari, with the Norman cathedral that was transformed into a Baroque building and the castle that was converted into a museum of Aeolian civilization are more examples. Then we have Acireale and Sciacca, spa cities rich with tradition; Marsala with its sweet wine, the gate built to celebrate the arrival of Garibaldi's troops, and the Phoenician island of Mozia. And then Piazza Armerina with its mosaics and the Norman Palio. And Modica, Scicli, Palazzolo del Barocco, Gagliano del Castello Ferrato, Mazara del Vallo, the hexagonal Grammichele, Sambuca-Zamut, Santo Stefano of the majolica tiles, Savoca of the mummies, Sortino with its honey and Maniace which remained under its feudal regime until just a few years ago. And the newest of all, Gibellina, another creation following an earthquake, the most recent in 1968. This list could go on and on. It makes one understand the reserve of the emigré who prefers to hold inside him that which he would like everyone to share.

THE PALERMO
OF THE CASSARO

36 top A bronze quadriga by Mario Rutelli adorns the top of the Politeama Garibaldi, designed by Damiani Almeyda during the 19th century.

36-37 The church of San Giovanni degli Eremiti was built during the Norman period by Islamic workers.

37 top View of Palermo with Monte Pellegrino behind.

37 bottom The Teatro Massimo was built between 1875 and 1897 by architects Giovan Battista and Ernesto Basile, father and son. Many buildings were pulled down to make way for it, including the church of San Giuliano with its massive dome.

38-39 The fountain of Piazza Pretoria was commissioned from Francesco Camilliani by Don Pietro di Toledo for his Florentine villa. It was purchased in 1578 by the Palermo Senate and placed in the popularly named "Chianu di la Curti."

40-41 *The* Vucciria *is the best known of Palermo's outdoor markets. It was depicted in several splendid paintings by Renato Guttuso and takes its name from the vucci (butchers) because it used to be the city's main meat market. Another market, which no longer exists, is*

remembered in Palermitan idioms, the Curtigghiu di li Raunisi *(courtyard of the Aragonese), in which tough commoners fought with sellers to obtain lower prices.* U curtigghiu di li Raunisi *is also the title of an anonymous farce and the first example of popular Sicilian theater before the* Mafiusi di la Vicaria, *by Rizzotto.*

CATANIA
BLACK WITH LAVA

42-43 The Bellini Garden is the largest green area in the city. It has trees, such as gigantic ficus, that are hundreds of years old, and various ducks and swans. There also used to be monkeys and even two elephants (the symbol of the city is an elephant called ḷiotru made of black lava). The first elephant, Menelik, was a gift to the city from King Umberto I of Italy in 1890 who had earlier received it from the ruler of Ethiopia, Menelik II. The animal is now stuffed and kept in the University Museum. The second, Tony, was given to the city by the Darix Togni circus in 1965.

43 top The statue of Ferdinand I Bourbon is by Antonio Calì. It was decapitated shortly after the arrival of Garibaldi's troops. The gallery of Palazzo Biscari can be seen behind; it faces onto Catania marina.

43 center View of the Baroque Benedictine monastery, rebuilt after the 1693 earthquake.

43 bottom Detail of the ornamental decorations of the facade of Palazzo Biscari, designed by Francesco Battaglia.

44-45 The domes of two Baroque Catanese churches: the snowy peak of Etna forms the backdrop.

THE WHITE CITY
OF SYRACUSE

46 Syracuse was founded in the second half of the 8th century BC by Corinthian colonists. Its continuous political and cultural influence culminated during the dynasty of the Dinomenids. During the reign of Hiero I the Syracuse court was visited by the most famous poets of the era, such as Simonides, Bacchylides, Pindar and Aeschylus. It reached the peak of its political power during the tyranny of Dionysius (between 406 and 367 BC) and then decline set in, marked by internal struggles, pressure from enemies and heavy foreign domination, the last being that of the Bourbons. It became part of the kingdom of Italy after Garibaldi captured Sicily and Naples with his 1000 "Redshirts." The picture shows moorings for fishing boats on the Nazario Sauro Riviera inside the city's smaller harbor.

47 The Greek theater, surrounded by stone quarries, is one of the largest and most perfect from antiquity. It was made from white stone by the architect Demekopos (also known as "Myrilla" – meaning unguent – as this was what was distributed to the public during its inauguration).
Syracuse was where Epicharmus, the father of Greek comedy, lived.

Along with Athens and Alexandria, Syracuse was one of the major centers of theatrical culture. It is said that Syracuse was where Aeschylus' tragedy The Persians was first shown. Aeschylus was also the author of The Etneans,which was written to commemorate the foundation of Etna by Hiero I and which first was performed in Syracuse in 476 BC.

MESSINA, DAUGHTER OF AN EARTHQUAKE

48 left This is an aerial view of Punta Faro, the tip of land that sticks out into the fish-filled waters of the Mediterranean towards mainland Italy.

48-49 Detail of the 16th-century fountain of Orion executed by Giovanni Montorsoli and Domenico Vanello, built to commemorate the construction of the city's first aqueduct. The fountain is one of the few ancient monuments to have survived the series of earthquakes that has hit the city over the centuries.

49 top View of the city center. The city was completely destroyed in 1908 by a violent earthquake. It was rebuilt in keeping with anti-seismic criteria but suffered further damage from heavy bombing during World War II.

CALTANISSETTA
CAPITAL OF SULPHUR

50 Caltanissetta was once the capital of the Sicilian sulfur industry, to which it has dedicated a museum. The world of those working in the sulfur mines was described in Ciaula Discovers the Moon, *a novella by Luigi Pirandello. The city is dominated by* the ancient castle of Pietrarossa, built as an Arab fortification and captured by the Norman count, Roger de Hauteville, in 1086. After chasing out the Saracens for good, Roger founded the Priory of San Giovanni, around which the city grew up.

51 Enna is the highest provincial capital in Europe. All of Sicily lies at its feet. It was from here that the Arab conquerors decided to divide Sicily into three political territories: the valley of Maraza, the valley of Demone, and the valley of Noto. Until 1927 the city was called Castrogiovanni, the Italian corruption of the Arab name Qasr Yannah which, in turn, was how the Saracens transcribed the Latin name of Castrum Hennae.

THE MOSAICS
OF PIAZZA

52-53 This is a series of photographs of the Roman Villa del Casale, in Piazza Armerina in the province of Enna. A series of excavations begun in 1929 by Paolo Orsi has uncovered several superb mosaics. The mosaics in living rooms, galleries, peristyles, courtyards and hot bath rooms on different levels of a slope are protected by plastic covers. Their beauty and the huge area they cover make Villa del Casale a unique monument.

54-55 Charming image of Piazza Armerina against a gloomy, stormy background. The city is also known for the Palio dei Normanni *(Norman horse race)* that takes place on August 15th. It celebrates the festival of the Madonna delle Vittorie (Virgin of the Victories*)*, whose standard was given to the inhabitants of the town by Count Roger for their contribution in expelling the Saracens.

BAROQUE
IBLA

56-57 Ibla was rebuilt in the Baroque style in 1730 after being destroyed in the 1693 earthquake. The picture shows the oldest section of the town where traces of prehistoric settlements have been found. Ibla stands in front of a hill where Ragusa is built, to which it is joined by a series of steps and bridges. The two districts used to be autonomous – Ibla was home to the ancient feudal nobility and Ragusa to the emerging economic classes – but they were unified in 1926 and a year later became the capital of the province.

TAORMINA
THE PEARL

58 left This fine aerial
view of Taormina with its
Greco-Roman theater
demonstrates how the city
deserves its description as
the "Pearl of the Ionian
Sea." Taormina's theater is
the second largest
classical theater in Sicily. It
was built by the Greeks on
the top of a hill and was
later enlarged and almost
completely rebuilt by the
Romans.

58-59 The Gulf of Naxos and Etna are the natural background to the ancient theater which the Romans turned into an amphitheater for gladiatorial fights. The remains of a small temple were found on the eastern side of the cavea.

59 top Taormina's attractive public gardens.

MOSAICS
ON THE COLUMNS

60-61 The cathedral of Monreale, built between 1172 and 1189, is a real work of Norman art. The interior of the three-nave basilica is decorated with Byzantine style mosaics, in particular the central apse with its splendid image of Christ Pantocrator. The cloister square dates from the 12th century; the pointed arches are supported by 228 twin columns, both decorated with mosaics or sculpted.

TRAPANI
AND THE SEA

62-63 The warm light of sunset veils the city of Trapani against the background of the Egadian islands. The city's maritime tradition is reflected in the Cappella dei Marinai (Sailors' Chapel) in the Santuario dell'Annunziata (Sanctuary of the Annunciation) and in the delicious dishes of steamed couscous served with an infinite variety of fish condiments.

THE NORMAN CITY OF CEFALÙ

64-65 Cefalù gets its name from a rock in the shape of a head that stands over the town. It was founded by the Greeks and became an independent diocese under the Normans. Roger II built many buildings and churches, including the Norman cathedral, one of Sicily's most beautiful. The excellent painting Portrait of an Unknown Man, *by Antonello da Messina, hangs in the Mandralisca Museum in Cefalù.*

THE SEA OF COLA PESCE

For those who were born in Sicily, going back is like returning to the maternal womb, protected from all outside interference, in an atmosphere made torpid by the humid warmth, where time passes slowly, measured by the comforting echo of a heartbeat. The island is a microcosm marked by incredibly rapid and violent vital processes, but it is also mysterious and ineluctable, where one is separated from reality and surrounded by an enormous mass of amniotic fluid. The fluid is the sea and the song of the surf is the sound of the mother's heartbeat; and as their rhythm is the indication of her mood, so the sea is both loved and hated. Its colors are simply enchanting: white with foam at Sciacca, violet at Trezza, dark blue in front of Palermo, lightest green at Brucoli, phosphorescent at Zingaro, and red where the sea-birds make their home in the marsh at Vindicari.

The sea to Sicilians is the gateway to the world but also from where invaders, merchants and pirates arrived. The coast is dotted with the ruins of look-out towers for the "Mammatraj," the terrible Turkish pirates named after the most ferocious, Mohammed Dragut. The memory of these pirates is so great that down the centuries even to the present day, Sicilian mothers frighten their restless children by telling them, "Look out, here comes the Mammatraju."

It was as a result of this fear that villages and towns began to be built inland on the hills out of sight of the sea, but on all the small islands that surround Sicily there were towns and cities where it was impossible to hide, whose histories are even more closely linked to the sea.

First, there are the Aeolian islands which one can reach at night using the volcano as a lighthouse. It used to guide sailors from far-off places who went there to purchase obsidian, the black and shiny volcanic glass that was used to make knives and arrow points and axe heads before iron was known. The ancient Mediterranean civilization was actually called an "obsidian civilization" and the Aeolian islands were at its center.

The most isolated is Alicudi, a lump of rock covered with heather and flailed by the wind. It is surrounded by deep blue water that used to be watched with apprehension from the *timpuni de' fimmini*, the shelter where the women fled when pirate ships were sighted.

Then there is Stromboli, with its black beach named Ficogrande, the *Sciara del fuoco* and Ginostra, bedecked with helichrysum and its satellite, Strombolicchio, which looks like a petrified ship with a figurehead in the shape of the head of an animal.

Vulcano is the island of medicinal herbs and of Venus' Pool; Salina was seen by the ancients as a woman sleeping among the waves who guards gigantic ferns, fields of camomile, thousand-year-old chestnut trees and Perciati of curdled lava in her bosom.

Filicudi is ringed by coral, has a prehistoric village that faces the warm southern wind and is known for its remarkable cliff named the *Scoglio della Canna*. The waters of Panarea are warmed by underwater geysers that look like the mouths of Hell. Offshore lie the four islets of Dattilo, Liscabianca, Liscanera and Basiliuzzo; the latter is home to jackdaws and seagulls and used to see the seasonal herding of the island's animal flocks.

Finally, there is Lipari, the kingdom of Liparo who left his crown to Aeolus, the husband of his daughter, to return to the continent. Lipari has white beaches, salt-works, a castle that stands on vitreous rock, and flows of obsidian and pumice stone. Lipari is also the island of Malvasia wine and the Dionysian cult of the theater for which a huge number of votive masks inspired by dramatic characters made from colored terracotta have been found by archaeologists. Lipari is always visible from the tops of the high mastheads on the boats of the swordfish fisherman in the Strait of Messina. The lookouts scrutinize the water for hours until they see the froth which indicates the courting dance of the fish when they pass in this area. Once sighted, the signal is given to harpoon them using the *dreffinere* (a special kind of harpoon) with long cables, then the fish are allowed to tire themselves out as they pull the boat, and the crew try to stick them before pulling them aboard. The swordfish hunt is relived in June each year for San Giovanni in a pantomime played out among the cliffs of Acitrezza. This is an ancient ritual that follows the dictates of popular magic in which the fishermen try in vain to catch their prey – the role of the fish is given to the most handsome and strongest boy in the village – but the fish does not just escape, he ends up tipping the boat over.

It is curious to know that a similar ceremonial pantomime is performed by aboriginal Australians, but this is no more than a sign that man is the same in the most arcane and intimate expression of his feelings all over the world.

The Pelagian islands are more greatly marked by their nearest continental neighbor, Africa, which has bequeathed them bronze-colored *coleoptera*, unwinged grasshoppers and strange lizards. In summer, sea turtles lay their eggs on these, the southernmost islands in Europe, and regina falcons arrive from Madagascar, so called because they were protected by edict by Queen Eleonora d'Arborea centuries ago. The smallest of the Pelagian islands is Lampione, then there is Linosa with its extinct volcanoes and the choral singing of the shearwaters and the yellow crickets.

Lampedusa was once Phoenician and later Roman. Its thick forests were filled with foxes, boar and small deer until 1839 when

it was sold by the Tomasi princes to Ferdinand II. He sent 120 colonists who were given rights to "free hunting and fishing" in addition to the possibility of using the trees; this led to the desertification of the island in just a few decades and to the transformation of its beauty into African landscapes, some of which are breathtakingly beautiful like the *Isola dei Conigli*, with its very light blue sea. Part African and part European, a pact was signed in 1221 for it to be administered jointly by Frederick II and the Emir of Tunis, Abbuissac, as well as its sister island *Bent el rion* (Arabic for daughter of the wind), which has been transformed into Pantelleria in Italian. The island boasts the *Sesi*, a group of magical megaliths created five thousand years ago by ancient inhabitants of the island, its *dammusi* (cool, ancient cubic houses), the Barbacane castle made from black lava, Venus' Mirror (a warm lake inside a crater), and the Point in the shape of an elephant's head drinking from the sea, with the ears flapping. When the flowers of the caper plants open to resemble wild orchids, the island is a real spectacle.

On the maps Ustica looks like a tiny round lentil like those cultivated by the farmers on its bare volcanic slopes. The name "Mount of the Turkish Guard" speaks volumes about the massacres of the Lipari colonists on Ustica and the island, after a long period spent housing a prison, has now been recognized as a chest of treasures: its fauna and flora and iridescent coastal caves have been protected in a marine reserve.

Lastly, there are the Egadi islands. Marettimo has great pink stone cliffs and immense caves with high-flown names; little Levanzo has cave drawings over ten thousand years old that show tuna fishing as it is still practiced on Favignana, Odysseus' island of goats. Favignana gets its name from the *favonio*, the wind that pushes these enormous, silent, silver fish into the nets. Favignana has always been linked to tuna fishing as can be seen by the splendid tuna processing plant built by Palermo architect Damiani Almeyda using tufa extracted from the same island and famous throughout the Mediterranean for its softness. The fish are lifted in the boats after the *occisa*, an equal armed struggle between man and the enormous king of the sea: maneuvering *ritenute* and *tradimenti* (ropes), the crew lift the heavy nets from the water to the sound of the *cialome*, the characteristic songs of the tuna fishermen:

> *Aya mola aya mola*
> *Gesù Cristu ccu' li santi*
> *Aya mola aya mola*
> *E lu santu Sarvaturi*
> *Aya mola aya mola*

The net of the death chamber, the last of the process, fills like an enormous sack inside the square formed by the boats.

> *Gnanzou*
> *San Cristofuru*
> *Gnanzou*
> *Granni e Grossu*
> *Gnanzou*

The net tightens as the water drains out.

> *Isa isa*
> *Zza' Monica 'n cammisa*
> *SPARA A TUNNINAAA!*

The tails of the tuna flail wildly like scythes, sending spray everywhere as the fish gasp for life. Then the crew guide these enormous fish with hooks on the tip of long poles towards the *crocc'a 'mmenzu* who pull them inside the black barges, dodging to avoid the lethal blows of the tails. The *occisa* takes place in an unreal atmosphere in which the participants are baptized by blood and salt water as though taking part in a cathartic pagan rite in which one is struck by the absence of the sacrificial victims' screams of agony. If the tuna could scream, tuna killing would have never taken place. Instead, the tuna fish business was perhaps Sicily's largest industry until the 19th century. There were twenty-one plants that treated the "sea pig" (it was called this because every part of it was used) in which the fish were cooked in enormous caldrons so that their meat could be tinned with olive oil. The tins were differently colored depending on which part of the fish was used: the soft belly, the dorsal zone (tuna proper), or the flanks and the tail. The same tuna fishermen were responsible for decapitating and cleaning out the insides of the fish as well as extracting the ovarian sacs of the females, which were sundried to make *botargo*. The rest of the sea-pig was left to steep in the *camposanto* (in the center of the tuna boat) from which oil was made that was used in foundries; then the dried residue was either turned into a flour to be used for animal feed or into a fertilizer. The Sicilian tuna boats were so important to the economy of the island that, during the tuna killing season, their owners and administrators could not be sent to prison. The "tuna-fish culture" also led to the construction of many lovely buildings, like the plants at Scopello and Marzamemi – the property of the Nicolaci di Villadorata family that lived in the palace with the corbels carved in the shape of lions, monsters, cherubs and pairs of winged horses. The new factories were built to replace the plant at Bafuto that had become unhealthy due to the malaria in the nearby marshes of Vindicari. Then there is the plant at Capo Passero, painted in a picture held in the Museum of Naples, a beautiful building in the Spanish style belonging to the princes of Bruno di Belmonte but erected in the 18th century by the curiously named Palermo baron Rau Xa Xa. This building is surrounded by fishermen's houses and dwarf palm trees. It stands beside the ruins of a Greek tuna processing plant and what is known as the "Pantano Marghella," a large natural salt-pan, because tuna plants always needed large quantities of salt.

The loveliest salt-works, now abandoned, are those at Vindicari and Marsala. They are home to a huge number of birds whose thousands of colors at sunrise and sunset testify to the magnificent variety of nature.

It was in Hector's Salt-works at Marsala, while the great blades of the windmills sang as they caught the wind and the last red rays of the sun were reflected in the large tanks in which the salt was "taking," that Don Turi Toscano, overseer of the salt-works, explained to me that one should not fear the sea. "Over there is Mozia which used to be Phoenician – there are still their tanks for preparing boats and drawings of panthers, but Garibaldi was there too. That's where they found a statue, I tell you, of Cola Pesce."

Cola Pesce is the main character in an infinite series of Sicilian legends. He was an ordinary boy but so good at swimming that he became a sort of deity, half man and half fish. With sufficient courage to dive down to get the crown that the king had thrown into the deep on a whim, and with a heart as big as the sea, he decided to stay in the underwater world and reign over one of the three columns on which Sicily rests so that it would not collapse. That is how he is portrayed in the statue dedicated to him in Catania, one of the most recent ones made in Sicily.

"After all this time down there," went on Don Turi, "Cola will by now have made friends with some large fish. And if I fall in the water, me that can't swim, he'll shout out: *Do me a favor as I can't go, there's Don Turi, go and get him and take him up.* That's why you shouldn't be afraid of the sea."

As you scan the horizon for ferocious pirates, the sea of Cola Pesce merges with the sky to become a single entity, allowing one's imagination to soar to far-off countries like the one where the Vuvitini live. The Vuvitini are men just knee-high to a grasshopper; they inhabit the part of the world where we place the soles of our feet, and watch us from the sloughs of the salt-pans.

71 top Ustica used to suffer terribly from pirate raids; today it is a sort of capital of the sea thanks to the institution of the "Golden Trident" awards, a near equivalent of the "Oscars" in the scuba-diving world.

THE SEVEN DAUGHTERS
OF KING AEOLUS

72-73 The stacks and the island of Vulcano, seen from Lipari. The Aeolian islands are a true paradise of limpid waters, luxuriant vegetation and natural monuments. The islands were at the center of ancient Mediterranean civilization because of their abundance of obsidian, a natural glass produced during the final stages of a volcanic eruption. The glass was used to make tools, knives, blades and small axes.

73 top A typical fishing boat pulled up out of the water on a beach in Salina.

73 center White fishermen's houses stretch out along the beach and slopes of the island of Vulcano.

73 bottom The central crater on Stromboli rises over 2953 feet above sea level.

74-75 The crater of Vulcano dominates the sea and islands below.

76-77 Salina was called Dydime by the ancients and was thought of as a woman lying asleep in the waves.

77 top Panarea was originally a volcanic island. Remains of Neolithic and Stone Age human settlements have been found here.

77 bottom Part of the cultivated area on Salina is used to grow capers. The flower of the spiny caper plant is similar to a wild orchid.

78-79 The pictures show boats moored in the harbor and fishermen mending their nets on Favignana. The ritual of the mattanza *(tuna killing)* is celebrated each year by the island's fishermen, as shown on the following pages. It is similar in nature to the contest between a bull and a matador.

80-81 *The duel between the tuna fishermen and the giant silver fish with scythe-like tail is a sort of metaphor of life and death in which man and his prey meet equally armed. There is no cruelty during the blood-spattered spray of the occisa but a battle fought for the spirit of survival. The ritual is an ancient one as shown by the wall-paintings in the Genovese Cave in Levanzo, which date from 12,000 BC. The battle takes place when the fish return from the Atlantic to the Mediterranean to breed.*

LINOSA, THE
PAINTED ISLAND

84-85 *On the left, colored houses on the island of Linosa, with giant terracotta pots of geraniums outside. On the right shows the lighthouse, with prickly pear plants in the foreground; these are one of the few plants that flourish on lava-based soil. Linosa is a volcanic island and even the walls that line the roads and paths are made from lava.*

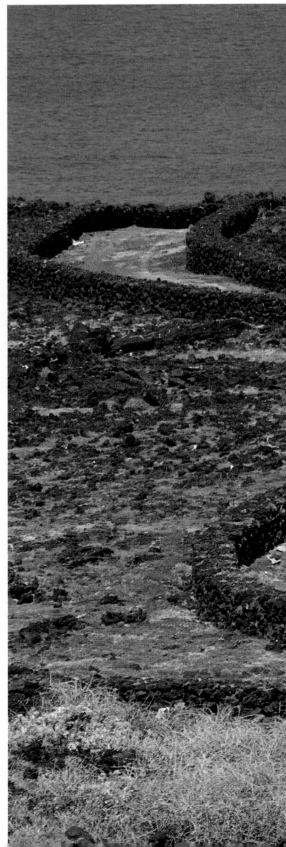

THE AFRICAN
PELAGIAN ISLANDS

86-87 Lampedusa was covered by forests that were home to foxes, boar and small deer until the mid-19th century, when King Ferdinand II sent 120 colonists to the island. In just a few decades they turned the rerdant land into a desert but Lampedusa's African landscapes are no less lovely, like the view of the Isola dei Conigli. The sea around Lampedusa is a turquoise blue and turtles now return to the beaches to lay their eggs.

THE LAND OF THE CAROB TREE

To me, the most authentic landscape in Sicily is the one that Piero Guccione painted of the infinite, uninterrupted background of sea and sky, as is appropriate to an island. Enzo Siciliano compared Guccione's pictures of the gullies of Ragusa to "a sorrowful melody with the carob trees in agony, worn away, the sadness of the stones at sundown and the glory of the corn-fields." It is a visible melody that can penetrate and educate the soul to the point, writes Bartels, that in Sicily "the last of the peasants has more feeling for beauty, truth and artistic expression than one of our orchestra conductor." Like Don Paolo from Sortino, who is one of the last craftsmen to carve wood into walking sticks, pipes and animal collars. Shepherds travel from a distance to allow him to choose the *cianciane* (bells) to attach to their animals' collars. Don Paolo's finely tuned ear enables him to select a small bell for each animal which harmonizes with those of the others in the herd so that the shepherd can recognize his herd by the melody it makes whenever it moves. Who knows which people over the millennia brought this custom with them for in Sicily nature too is an overlay of cultures. Almost all the plants chosen to be a symbol of the island have been imported: the vine, the olive, the almond and the pistachio by the Greeks, citrus fruits and the mulberry by the Arabs, and the aloe and the prickly pear by the Spanish after the discovery of America.

And it is surprising that among the *cuiri alleri* (bushes) of the broom on the slopes of Etna, a northern tree like the birch grows and that there is a Sicilian variant known as *arvulu cruci cruci* in the village of Polizzi Generosa. In this land of contrasts, we find African dwarf palms and the beech that grows on the slopes of the volcano and on the Madonie and Nebrodi hills. Every type of plant or tree that grows in Sicily has a close link with the religiousness, ceremonies, legends and medicines of the people. The Sicilian birch is shown with Jupiter on a coin of Etna; papyrus was used until the 18th century as an ornament for religious ceremonies; the old people of San Vito Lo Capo and Porto Palo plait baskets and elegant fans using the *curina* (heart) of the dwarf palm; and the whole of the almond tree is used – like the tuna and the pig – to create oils, essences, sweets, wood, charcoal slack and even a soft soap. Crossing the Sicilian landscape, the traveler is struck by the expanses of low, supported vines, florid in the land of Dionysus, used to produce the white wines of Alcamo and Etna, the generous reds of the volcano, the Cerasuolo of Vittoria and dessert wines to accompany philosophizing or idle gossip, such as the Malvasia of Lipari, the muscats of Pantelleria, Noto and Syracuse, and Marsala that one can taste even with one's eyes. "Is this wine which smiles below the froth? Or carnelian

topped by a row of pearls?," wrote the medieval Arab poet Hamdis when remembering the wine of Noto, his birthplace.

The presence of the green, orange and yellow citrus orchards on the slopes of Etna is announced by the perfume of the orange blossoms. The trees bring forth fruit that look like small suns able to brighten the greyest day or give blood and life back to a pale child.

The wheat is the child of the summer but is then changed into loaves so elaborate they look like lacework at the festival of San Giuseppe. The perfumed herb, basil, is another product of the heat and on June 24th is used to "*sancire i comparaggi*" (used to celebrate a special bond between the father and the godfather of a child) in enormous terracotta containers tied with a red ribbon. The sun also serves to dry the tomatoes that hang in great red bunches on the lime-coated walls of the houses in Trapani, and to bring the peppers and eggplants to the right size and maturity to make *caponata*, the bittersweet dish that is the gastronomic version of Palagonian taste. The green meadows, more numerous than one might think, are the grazing land for the musical flocks of Don Paolo. I remember him in a farmhouse with *paralupi,* a fig leaf in one hand and illuminated by a ray of sunshine that entered between some loose tiles, reciting prayers before a caldron for *tuma, primosale, cannistrato* and *pecorino* cheeses. He said three *pateravegloria* to the ricotta cheese, skimming it religiously with a terracotta cup, then baptized it with the nectar provided by the master honeymaker from Sortino, Don Giuseppe Blancato. Then there are the thousand-year-old Saracen olive trees that have seen and produced so much.

People who abandon their fields always keep a few olive trees for themselves to make oil for their family's use; it is always unique in its taste and smell. But there are other extremely old trees, like the "Hundred Horse Chestnut" which got its name, it is said, when Queen Joanna of Aragon and her entire retinue took shelter there from a storm. Almost four thousand years old and 171 feet in circumference, the chestnut stands in Sant'Alfio and used to contain "a house in which there was an oven for drying chestnuts, hazelnuts and almonds," according to Houel. Despite the public image that Sicily has of being a bare and barren land, it boasts 521 acres of oaks, cork, holm-oaks and chestnut trees on the Nebrodi, Madonie, Caronie, Iblei and Erei hills, and on Etna, in the ancient hunting grounds of the kings such as Ficuzza wood, and in the forest at Santo Pietro where for centuries the craftsmen of Caltagirone got the wood they used to heat the ovens to bake their pottery.

Sicily has another treasure up in the hills: water. The Simeto

and Alcantara rivers have their sources in the same area and have worked at creating their own colossal Palagonian works of art over the millennia: extraordinary ravines carved out of ancient lava beds which, in the case of the Alcantara, drop dozens of feet between the waterfall and the rapids. As it washed away the rock, the river has formed fantastic figures which seem almost to come to life at sunset and dance to the sound of a pipe organ in a representation of primordial chaos. The Arabs used this fantastic river as a breeding ground for crocodiles, as they did in the Abbas (the Oreto) in the province of Palermo and in the Anapo around Syracuse. The latter has something else in common with Alcantara: towering over it is an immense and extraordinary rock. This is Pantalica, the sacred mountain of the Siculi tribe, that stands in the midst of gigantic plane and oleander trees. It is an immense open-air cathedral that has stood for millennia while the river murmurs its eternal prayer. Pantalica is also linked for me to the memory of an authentically regal gesture made by Prince Charles of Britain some years ago when the area was still in the charge of the Forestry Commission; wanting to pay homage to this magnificent monument, he cleared up some of the waste paper thoughtlessly left by tourists too obtuse to recognize the holiness of the spot. This was a reconciliatory gesture for how certain monarchs have treated nature in Sicily. It was the English ambassador, Lord Hamilton, who recorded in his journal after accompanying Ferdinand, the first king of the Two Sicilies, on a hunting trip, how in eight days in Ficuzza wood, the gentlemen of the court had killed "a thousand deer, a hundred boar, three wolves and so very many foxes." He emphasized how the hunt had been "a massacre and not true sport." It is hardly surprising that there is no longer any trace of these animals in Sicily, with the exception of the fox, and they are having to be reintroduced to certain wooded areas.

One such place is the Zingaro, one of the loveliest nature reserves on the island and where Uzzo Cave is located. This is the cave that contained remains of men, deer, boar and bears that lived ten thousand years ago. There are 3954 hundred acres of wild and bare land, reached through the track of a road that was never completed. It used to be such a poverty stricken area that the people used to scrape the ash trees for something to keep them from starvation. Imagine a petrified white snow on a sea like an enormous jewel, beneath an African sky that hasn't seen the path of a golden eagle for twenty years. But the small Bonelli's eagle and the *forbiciazze* (fork-tailed kites) are still there. The golden eagle has returned, on the other hand, to the mountain *par excellence*, Etna, or *jebel* (mount), as the Arabs called it, as though it were the only mountain in Sicily.

Orazio Nicoloso is not an Etna guide but he has trained many. He may be the man who knows the volcano best. Having climbed the mountain on foot together, we waited for dawn in a recess in the central crater, heated by boiling lava from a few feet down. We told each other stories about Etna and chatted about the locals, who do not see the volcano as a devil but rather as a strict father. Finally, we turned from the crater to watch the sun rise in the clean, transparent air. The shadow of Etna was projected right across Sicily with its tip stretching to some imprecise point between Palermo and Trapani.

This immense volcano began its life over half a million years ago when there was originally just a large gulf in its place. The lava began to flow under the sea until Etna itself appeared, growing higher with each eruption. The Siculi considered Etna a god whom they called Adranon. They built and dedicated a temple to him surrounded by enormous forests and watched over by a thousand sacred dogs that savaged those with bad intentions but escorted the faithful. Some say that the dogs were Cirnecos – small, elegant Sicilian hunting dogs like greyhounds – with pointed ears and similar to the "Pharoah's dogs" probably imported from Africa by Phoenician merchants who traded with the Sicilian cities on the banks of the Simeto river. Sicilian Greeks showed the Cirnecos on their coins, and they were the only dogs that Moslems would touch as they considered all others impure. Their skill in the hunt over the sharp *sciare* (cold lava flows) induced the peasants of Etna to keep this breed pure for centuries.

But there are other animals that are also typically Sicilian, such as the strong and agile Sanfratellano horse or the *modicani* cattle that are enclosed by *muretti a siccari* (dry walls) in the shade of immense carob trees, true monuments of nature. The carob is the best representation of the Sicilian peasant. It has firm, solid roots able to ensure survival in dry and rocky ground, huge thick evergreen leaves that give shade and cool in the torrid Sicilian heat, and poor quality fruit that is used to brighten stalls on festival days.

It is a strong and generous tree.

94-95 These pictures show the harvesting of the plants that are considered the symbols of the island – vines, olives and oranges – yet all of them were originally imported in various epochs by different colonists and invaders. The most recent were the prickly pear and the aloe, which were imported by the Spanish after the conquest of America. Native plants and trees include the birch, the beech, dwarf palms, the carob and fir trees. In certain inland mountain villages – like the snow-covered one on pages 98-99 – the temperature is cool enough to allow these northern trees to survive.

96-97 A typical Sicilian scene; a farmer and his donkey on rocky ground, where the prickly pear and flowers flourish.

ETNA,
A STRICT FATHER

100-101 Etna is not considered to be a destroyer by the people that live on the slopes but rather a strict father. It was here that many European travelers visiting Sicily in the 18th and 19th centuries began to understand the sense of the quiet contrasts that characterize the island. The German, Johann Heinrich Bartels, noted

how "the most delicate vegetation grows on blocks of spent fire." This immense volcano began life over half a million years ago when there was only a wide gulf in its place. The lava started to pour out from under the sea until, eruption after eruption, Etna emerged and continued to rise. The Siculi, some of the island's first inhabitants, considered the volcano to be a god whom they named Adranon, the lord of fire and war, and dedicated a temple to him surrounded by enormous forests and protected by a thousand sacred dogs.

102-103 These pictures show both the destructive power of the lava and the faith of the people. Some eruptions are considered to have been stopped after processions were held of simulacra or the reliquaries of saints, such as the veil of St. Agatha, the patron saint of Catania. More recently, Etna has been the object of study by scientific researchers and by the Civil defense, seeking ways of diverting or stopping lava flows. In 1983, the world's first experiment to divert a lava flow was carried out (although attempts had been made since 1669 by ardimentosi brave men armed with picks and clubs) and in 1992, Professor Franco Barberi, President of the National Group of Volcanologists, successfully concluded "Operation Thrombosis," in which lava flows were encouraged to flow from high altitude caves down the same paths as flows from previous months. But Etna is also a laboratory of natural history, covered with plants up to a certain altitude, then home to the "holy thornbush" shown on pages 104-105.

PROTAGONISTS IN THE FESTIVALS

The great popular tradition of the Baroque in Sicily might be thought to derive from the inherent theatricality of the style in that it is able to satisfy the ambition of peoples who wish to be protagonists after so many invasions and subjugations. Protagonism is one of the less obvious, but strong, qualities of Sicilians – whether it is a good or bad point depends on your point of view. Bartels noted it when he wrote his version of the observation made by the Syracusan Saverio Landolina Nava, "the enthusiasm of these men for festivals turns them into madmen, seeing that they have no opportunity for being heroes." Such an opportunity arises with the colossal effort required to carry the statue of St. Philip Syriac at breakneck speed down the slope towards Calatabiano or when the litter of St. Agatha is pulled up the steep San Giuliano hill in Catania, which is the slope of a volcano that has been extinct for centuries. These are collective efforts; where protagonism is really evident is in the festival of Sant'Alfio di Trecastagni.

The night of May 9th is filled with the agonizing cries of the *nudi* (men wearing just a pair of breeches and a red sash around their chest and women dressed but shoeless) who carry the giant candles on litters on their shoulders to the cathedral dedicated to the "three innocent lambs" (the saint actually had two brothers, Filadelfo and Cirino, who were martyred with him in a dungeon at Militello, though the eager crowd is there just for Alfio). This spring festival in the province of Catania was so important that in the 18th century women used to insert clauses in their marriage contract obliging their husbands to accompany them to it each year. It was also an opportunity to buy garlic, straw hats, tambourines and, more recently, watch the parade of Sicilian carts decorated with heroic scenes of the paladins of France, as described by story-tellers. Like in so many other festivals, the culmination of Sant'Alfio was *i giochi di fuoco* (a spectacle using fire). There are all types of such spectacles in Sicilian festivals; for example, the ones similar to those at Marina di Palermo enthusiastically described by Houel as "an enchanted wood prepared for the triumph of Amphitrite," and others less extinct. These pyrotechnical spectacles replaced the *mosaici di fuoco* (fire mosaics) like the one still to be seen at the festival of San Giacomo at Caltagirone on the steps of the church of Santa Maria del Monte, and large ritual bonfires like the one on which King Burlone is burned at the end of the carnival in Acireale each year. This is thought to be Sicily's most beautiful carnival festival, with its gigantic allegorical floats, masked groups, bands that parade in a splendid Baroque setting, and the huge crowds equalled only by those at Sciacca during its carnival. Nevertheless, both the tradition of burning King Burlone and that of the papier-maché floats are relatively recent. The only "giants" used to be Mata and Grifone, the mythical founders of Messina whose floats tour the city on August 15th. More akin to an allegorical float was the *Varca*, a boat without a bottom made from papier maché on which men dressed as sailors toured the streets "fishing" for sausages, pork jelly, macaroni and wine in an amusing "alms collection."

Ancient carnivals centered around the figure of "Nannu," a puppet of an old man whose death was ritually announced by the *vecchia di li fusa* (the old woman with the spindle), a remembrance of the myth of the three Fates. After the excess of Carnival, an entertaining outlet for an extremely rigid society, huge tables were laid, *carnascialate* (carnival jokes) were played in which barons and doctors (called *Pisciacalamari*) were made fun of and, in Catania, the *dirittu di li 'ntuppateddi* allowed women, when masked, all sorts of liberties. "Nannu" died to the wails of the hired mourners but always with the certainty of rising again the following year, like in ancient myths. This is recalled in a verse of the *repitu* (the chorus of two voices in the hired mourners): "*Morsi lu Nannu, lu nannu muriu. Ppi' 'nautru annu nun pipita cchiu.*" (Nannu is dead, Nannu has died. He will not return for another year). Before dying, King Burlone had made a will, usually rather obscene, reporting all the sins of the people which he would take with him in his role as a scapegoat.

The most authentic modern-day version of Carnival in Sicily is certainly that of the *Mastru di campu* (Master of the Field) at Mezzojuso, a parody of the siege of Solunto Castle, where Queen Blanche of Navarre, the widow of King Martin and the deputy ruler of the kingdom, had taken refuge from Count Bernardo Cabrera whose love for Blanche was unrequited. The festival, which much resembles the spirit of the *Opera dei Pupi* (Puppet Theater), has three characters: the King, the Queen and the Master (also called the General, who is tall, lanky and wears a red mask). A *tubbiana* (troop of masked characters) made up of devils, wizards, peasants, shepherds, ministers and cuirassiers on horseback, all in 15th-century Spanish costume, surrounds the main characters. The King, the Queen and their ministers take their places on the platform of the castle, then the Master arrives on horseback to a drum roll, surrounded by soldiers and barons. He makes signs that show he is in love with the Queen. He then sends his declaration of war to the King and the battle begins: with his sword unsheathed he attacks with theatrical gestures one, two, three times but the King wounds him in a duel forcing him into a theatrical *caruta* (fall) from the castle walls as the Queen faints. But the Master, restored

to life, takes command of his troops again, the cannons fire and he succeeds in scaling the castle walls to reach the Queen and declare his love. Chased away once more, he turns to craftiness. He bribes the enemy soldiers, captures the King and, arm in arm, he parades with the Queen to the sound of music, dances and nursery rhymes: *"Purra, purra papirribbella. Bichiri, bichiri, papirribbella."* It is very reminiscent of traditional Carnival when Pulcinella plays tarantellas and fasolas on his lute with other masked characters with *friscaletti, viulini, scattagnetti, tammurini e tammureddi, e corni e brogne* (whistles, violins, tambourines and tambourels, and horns and shells) like in the *banni d'è mascariati* (bands) which still exist in Sicily. There are the band of Umbrillara from Santa Teresa di Riva in the province of Messina and the shabby band from the Villaggio Santa Maria Goretti, the most popular in Catania, which plays march tunes during the rugby matches of the Amatori rugby team. The latter shows the best side of a city raised on the enjoyment of thumbing its rose at others and realizing dreams from nothing.

The *pecchi* (the names of these musical players) are as carnivalesque as any Sicilian masked character: Pecura janca, Cacaniuru, Sasizza and Furmagginu against Tofalu, Nofiu Taddarita and, of course, Peppi 'Nnappa, the most lovable character also because he is so well known by spectators of the *Opera dei Pupi*.

After Carnival comes Easter which is maybe the largest of all festivals in Sicily. It is filled with contrasting features; for example, the Devil is part of the procession in Prizzi in the province of Palermo. A medieval legend tells of a group of demons that invaded the village and encouraged the inhabitants to sin and for centuries now, the *abballu di li diavuli* (the dance of the devils) has been relived during Holy Week; young men dressed in red outfits, large red masks and goatskins that drape down over their shoulders tour the streets looking for victims from whom they can demand money for something to drink. Death tours with them dressed in a yellow outfit and mask and armed with a loaded crossbow.

Devils and Death in yellow are also to be seen in Adrano in the province of Catania, where since the 18th century, they have been the main characters in a holy play which is performed on Easter Day between the Norman castle and the church. The plot is simple and even trivial: the forces of evil – Lucifer, Ashtaroth, Beelzebub and Death – want to possess Humanity but Archangel Michael intervenes and frees them. Humanity and Michael are impersonated by children who wear white clothes while the devils are dressed in black, monstrous outfits. Even more ugly is Death who, realizing that he will not be able to vanquish Humanity, breaks his arrow and throws it into the crowd. The people all scrabble for the parts, which are considered to be lucky charms.

Demons are also an element at San Fratello, where the streets are filled with "Jews" on the Wednesday and Friday of Holy Week. Like the devils in Prizzi, the Jews are allowed to do pretty much as they like; it seems that in the past, armed with swords, trumpets and *discipline* (whips), these "Jews" actually perpetrated vendettas.

There are also mystical spectacles that originated from medieval *laudi* (hymns of praise) lyrical in the beginning but later transformed into dramatic modes. *Lodate* (praises) and *lamenti* (laments) are one of the rare polyphonic works of the Sicilian oral tradition sung by the male choirs of various monastic confraternities. The lyrics are taken from episodes of the Gospels and are mainly in Sicilian dialect though some are in Italian or a rough liturgical Latin; they deal with the death and resurrection of Christ. Out of these lyrical dramas, groups representing Martyrs, Mysteries, Casazzas and Devotions have evolved. Processions of the Mysteries, (a group of sculptures inspired by the Gospel), parade at Trapani, Marsala, Caltanissetta and Enna. At Enna, the hooded *confradias* (confraternities) march to the rhythm of the *tabbala*, a huge drum, while at Caltanissetta ten musical bands each perform a funeral march on the Thursday before Easter, disturbed by *troccule* (wooden boards which youngsters strike). On Easter Day, the bands perform lively marches at the *lu 'ncontru* (meeting) between the statues of the Grieving and the Risen Christ. This is the most joyful moment of the festival because the Savior is not really the protagonist in this festival. As Sciascia wrote, "… he had died … but his mother was still alive: grieving, enclosed in her black mantle of heavy grief … The true drama was hers: earthly, physical." This is confirmed by the dialogue given by Favara between Mary and the blacksmith who is making the preparations for the crucifixion, wracked by grief. The people therefore feel close to the role played in the divine sacrifice of the Madonna to such a point that, in the poignant presentation at Burgio, she becomes the unquestioned protagonist of the drama.

On Easter Day, the people rejoice for Mary when the gigantic figure of St. Peter tours the streets of the "Giunta" in Caltagirone in search of the Virgin to announce the Resurrection. He then hurries to meet the Risen Christ, who stands between two Jews, called *Chicchittu* and *Nancittu* by the people. The joyful pealing of bells is mixed with the equally spirited trills of the terracotta *friscaletti* (whistles), the humble toy of Sicilian children, sold on the festival stalls at Easter.

109 The deeds of Orlando, Rinaldo, Angelica and Emperor Charlemagne made a great impression at a time when cinema and television did not exist and the theaters were almost exclusively the privilege of the rich. Today, the great families of puppet masters have almost all disappeared with the exception of the Cuticchio in Palermo and the Napoli in Catania.

THE CARTS
OF THE PALADINS

110-111 *The exploits of the paladins of France are relived on the sides of traditional Sicilian carts even if they are kept in museums like that of Aci Sant'Antonio in the province of Catania. Occasionally they are paraded in public, as happens at the festival of Sant'Alfio in Trecastagni.*

THE BATTLE OF THE MASTER OF THE FIELD

112-113 *Epic themes are the subject of the pantomime* Mastru di campu *(Master of the Field)* in Mezzojuso in the province of Palermo. This performance is perhaps the most authentic of popular Sicilian carnivals.

The show parodies the siege of the castle of Solunto where Queen Blanche of Navarre (widow of King Martin and deputy head of the country) had hidden from the Count of Modica, Bernardo Cabrera. A troop of

masked characters, typical of carnivals from the past, moves around the main characters of the pantomime: the Master of the Field (who succeeds in taking the castle after bribing the guards), the King and the Queen.

CARNIVAL TIME
AT ACIREALE

114-115 *"The best Carnival in Sicily," with allegorical papier-maché floats, vehicles covered with flowers and figures made using oranges and other citrus fruits, is by definition the Carnival at Acireale, which attracts a huge number of visitors each year. The lovely Baroque city is literally invaded by tourists who often take advantage of*

the visit for a "health holiday," spending the morning in the spa and the afternoon to late evening in the streets watching the parades of floats, masked groups and lively musical bands. A similar festival takes place in Sciacca near Agrigento but the tradition of allegorical floats and that of burning King Burlone at the end of the event are relatively recent. The personification of the ancient Sicilian carnival is "Nannu," a puppet that dies as a scapegoat after having taken on the collective sins of the people.

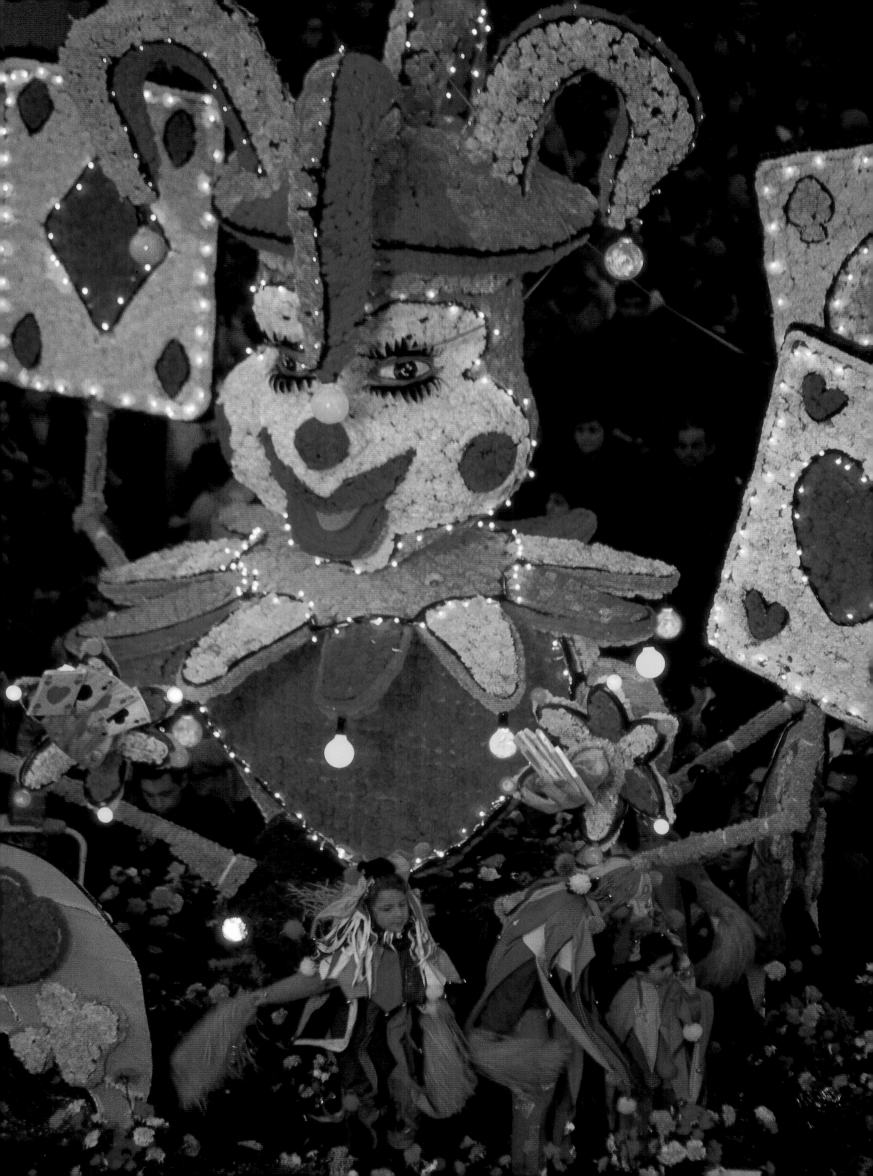

THE DEVIL
BEHIND THE ALTAR

118-119 Devils are the main characters in the Easter celebration at Adrano in Catania. This takes place in the main square below the Norman castle. The plot of the "Diavolata" is simple and even trivial: the forces of evil represented by Lucifer, Ashtaroth, Beelzebub and Death (this last in yellow) attempt to take possession of Humanity after the death of Christ – but with the Resurrection, Archangel Michael frees Humanity.

THE
CONFRATERNITIES
OF ENNA

120-121 The Good Friday procession in Enna is special because of the many confradies *(confraternities) that parade in hoods. The procession marches to the rhythm of the* tabbala *(large drum). During the procession the Black Madonna of Enna is devotedly carried on the shoulders of the faithful.*

THE DAYS
OF THE JEWS

122-123 San Fratello is a village in the Nebrodi hills where the inhabitants speak a strange Gallic-Italian dialect. Holy Week here is characterized by the presence of "Jews" who wear red hoods and jackets and carry swords, whips and tinplate trumpets. They are allowed to do whatever they like on the Wednesday and Friday before Easter. The same happens at Prizzi in the province of Palermo where the Abballu di li diavuli (Dance of the Devils) is relived each year. Young men in red outfits and masks and wearing a goatskin over their shoulders tour the streets in search of "victims" forced to give them money to spend on drink.

A SPANISH
EASTER

124-125 Night-time pictures taken of Holy Week in Caltanissetta, one of the loveliest celebrations on the island. These cerimonies had

their origin in medieval hymns of praise that were turned from lyric into dramatic and which were strongly promoted during the period of the Spanish domination. "Martyrs," "Mysteries," "Casazzas" and "Devotions" came into being; they still survive in many other towns in Sicily.

"LI SCHETTI"
OF CALATAFIMI

126-127 One of the most curious popular festivals in Sicily is the Festival of the Crucifix in Calatafimi, the small town in the province of Agrigento known mostly for the Battle of May 15, 1860, won by Garibaldi against, the Bourbon troops. The festival, also known as "di li schetti," has a parade of men dressed in black carrying rifles. The parade undoubtedly extols the "heroic" component of Sicilian festivals that was highlighted in the 19th century by the German Johann Heinrich Bartels when, in contemplation of the Syracusan Saverio Landolina, he wrote, "the enthusiasm of these men for festivals turns them into madmen, seeing that they have no opportunity for being heroes."

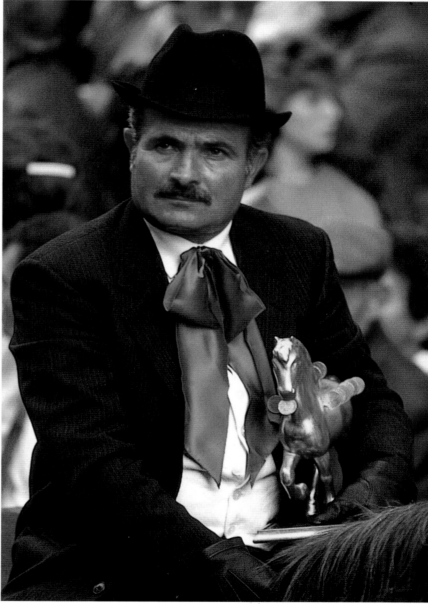